T★H★E
NORTH CENTRAL STATES

DANIEL JACOBSON

A GROLIER COMPANY

FRANKLIN WATTS
NEW YORK★LONDON★TORONTO★SYDNEY★1984
A FIRST BOOK

Maps by Vantage Art, Inc.

Cover photographs courtesy of:
Kansas Department of Economic Development;
Chrysler Corporation; Ruth Crisman; Shostal

Photographs courtesy of: The Bettmann Archive:
pp. 3, 35, 36; Union Pacific Railroad: p. 4; Ford
Motor Company: pp. 6, 60, 81; North Dakota Tourism Promotion: pp. 13, 77; U.S. Department of Agriculture: p. 14, 46; American Museum of Natural History: p. 17; New York Public Library Picture Collec-
tion: pp. 22, 28, 56; Library of Congress: p. 30; How-
ard W. Sawhill: p. 40; USDA Soil Conservation Service: pp. 43, 45; Boston Museum of Fine Arts: p. 51;
Michigan Travel Bureau: pp. 55, 75; Kansas Department of Economic Development: p. 63; United Press
International: p. 65; Chicago Historical Society: p.
69; Illinois Department of Tourism: p. 70; Wisconsin Division of Tourism: p. 76;

Library of Congress Cataloging in Publication Data

Jacobson, Daniel, 1923-
The north central states.

(A First book)
Includes index.
Summary: Discusses the history, geography,
agriculture, industry, cities, and future of
"The American Heartland."
1. Middle West—Juvenile literature.
[1. Middle West] I. Title.
F597.J35   1984   977   83-19789
ISBN 0-531-04731-8

CONTENTS

THE
NORTH CENTRAL
STATES

INTRODUCTION: THE AMERICAN HEARTLAND

Shortly after the Revolutionary War, and especially after the War of 1812, Americans began to move west in great numbers. The chief attractions were cheap land and freedom. On foot and in Concord wagons New Englanders moved overland into New York and Pennsylvania; on flatboats they continued their journeys down the Ohio River to Ohio and beyond. Virginians moved west by way of the Great Valley through Cumberland Gap, into Kentucky and then north to the Ohio River settlements. North and South Carolinians were moving into Tennessee. Georgians had their eyes on Creek Indian lands in Alabama.

Americans were not alone in the westward movement. Cheap land and freedom attracted foreigners as well. French settlers had established Gallipolis on the Ohio River before the turn of the eighteenth century; after a short stay in Kentucky, Swiss winemakers moved into southeastern Indiana in 1804 to found Vevay; and an English settlement was built even farther west, near the Wabash River in southeastern Illinois in 1818. Pioneers were leaving the forests for the tall bluestem grasses and the big sky of the prairie.

Newspaper accounts, emigrant guide books, letters from western travelers, mineral discoveries, and new means of transportation continued to beckon Americans west. With the opening of the Erie Canal in 1825 and the rapid growth of steamboat navigation on the Great Lakes, New Yorkers began to move into Michigan Territory. When lead was "discovered" (the Indians and the French had known of lead's existence for many years) near Galena, Illinois, Americans moved quickly into the lead mining areas of Illinois, Iowa, and neighboring Wisconsin. The Mississippi River led settlers into Minnesota and squatters (those who settle on land without having title to it) occupied prairie lands in distant Kansas and Nebraska. Before long little towns began to rise on the western prairie. Leavenworth, Lawrence, and Topeka, in Kansas were all created in 1854. And towns began to appear in Nebraska and the Dakotas. There was simply no holding the westward tide.

Meanwhile, behind the advancing frontier, the land was filling up. Ohio's population had increased from just under 600,000 in 1820 to nearly 2,000,000 in 1850. Indiana could boast an increase from 150,000 in 1820 to nearly 1,000,000 in 1850. Illinois had made gains from 55,000 to over 900,000 in the same period.

And the landscape itself was changing. Rail lines were being built, uniting the eastern prairies with the East and South. Cincinnati, Cleveland, Indianapolis, Detroit, and Chicago were emerging as important rail centers. Farmers, using John Deere's new steel plow, corn planters, and row cultivators and Cyrus McCormick's reaper were building a new agriculture on the prairie land. There

Main Street in Ellsworth, Kansas,
during early settlement days

were fields of wheat, corn, barley, and hay as far as the eye could see. Cattle, sheep, and hogs were being raised.

By the late nineteenth century a prosperous Corn Belt was already in place, stretching from central Ohio to eastern Nebraska. Early in the twentieth century a winter wheat region was to mature in central Kansas and Nebraska, and a spring wheat region in eastern Minnesota, the eastern Dakotas, and in the prairie provinces of Canada.

The timber, copper, and iron ore resources of the Upper Great Lakes attracted settlers to the Upper Peninsula of Michigan and to northern Wisconsin and Minnesota. The rich iron ores were sent down the lakes to meet Michigan limestone, and Pennsylvania and Illinois coal to make steel. In East Chicago, the Inland Steel Corporation built a large plant. In 1905 the United States Steel Corporation began construction of its even larger plant, at what was to become Gary, on the Indiana dunes. Youngstown, Steubenville, Cleveland, Lorain, and Canton-Massilon would all emerge as important steel-producing centers.

Meanwhile Ransom E. Olds, Henry Ford, and others were beginning to set the world on wheels. The curved dash runabout—the first car to carry the name *Oldsmobile*—was already on the road in 1900. Henry Ford would build his famous Model T in 1908. By 1917, 184 companies were making passenger cars and another 145 were making delivery cars and trucks. Detroit and its surrounding communities of Pontiac, Flint, Lansing, and Jackson, and Windsor, Ontario, in Canada would become the automobile

*The building of an extensive network
of railroads encouraged settlement
in the American Heartland.*

capital of the world and a part of the greater American manufacturing region.

The American Heartland—Ohio, Indiana, Illinois, Michigan, Wisconsin, Minnesota, Iowa, Missouri, Nebraska, Kansas, South Dakota, and North Dakota—was booming. During World Wars I and II, blacks from the South, in ever-growing numbers, moved into the Heartland's cities to take jobs in the defense industries. Many became permanent residents. Chicanos, too, moving north with the crops, from Texas to the Dakotas, also decided to spend their lives in the American Heartland. The population soared. By 1960 over 51,000,000 people were living in the American Heartland; by 1980 the number was nearly 59,000,000, one quarter of the entire population of the United States.

But there were troubles on the horizon. High energy costs had increased inflation. High interest rates had made it difficult to buy new homes and consumer goods. Foreign cars, particularly from Japan and Germany, were making deep inroads in the American marketplace. By the late 1970s and early 1980s the growing threat of depression lingered over the American Heartland. Hundreds of thousands of steel and automobile workers were thrown out of work. Plants closed. The unemployment lines lengthened. Michigan, deeply involved in the production of automobiles, was particularly hard-hit. Unemployment there topped 17 percent; Illinois, Ohio, Indiana, and Wisconsin were not far behind. There were problems, too, in the Heartland's farm areas. Incomes dropped sharply, and many farmers lost their farms. Americans began to leave the Heartland for the Sunbelt states of

*Henry Ford in a forerunner
of his famous Model T*

the South and Southwest, and other areas where employment opportunities were better.

Distress in the heart of America—will it last? Can the American Heartland recover? What are the region's weaknesses and what are its strengths? What does the future hold for the American Heartland?

☆ 1 ☆

THE LAND

Level land, a fine climate, a varied natural vegetation and animal life, excellent soils, a fine array of minerals, and an abundant water supply played important roles in the development of the North Central States.

TERRAIN

The American Heartland is a flat to gently-rolling land area, shaped by the glaciers of long ago. The glaciers planed off the hilltops and filled in the gorges and deep valleys. They scooped out the beds of the Great Lakes and deposited glacial drift 100 feet (30.48 m) deep over the land surface. In the driftless area (southwestern Wisconsin and nearby Minnesota, Iowa, and Illinois), untouched by the glaciation, the land is hilly and rugged. And there are hilly and rugged lands in the Black Hills of the Dakotas and in the Missouri Ozarks. There is high ground in Kansas and Nebraska and in the iron ranges of Michigan, Wisconsin, and Minnesota. But, for the most part, the American Heartland is a level land suitable for the plow and for modern machine agriculture.

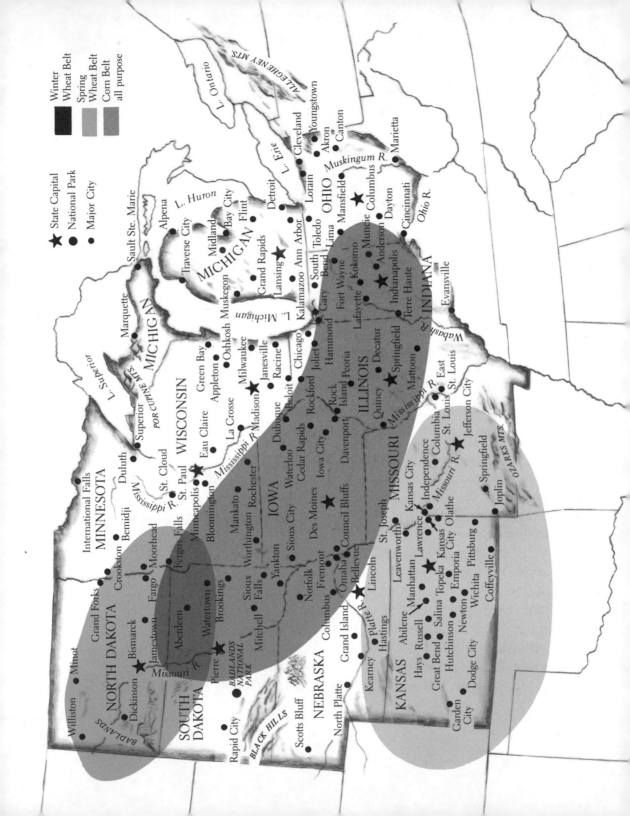

CLIMATE

The climate is an ideal one for farming. Hot summers with bright sunshine and moderate rainfall—ideal for growing corn—are typical of the American Heartland. Winters are cold, often severe, and snowfall is heavy. At Xenia, Ohio, the July average temperature is 75° F; the January average temperature, 30°F. Xenia receives 37 inches (93.98 cm) of precipitation each year; the growing season (the dates between the last killing frost in spring and the first killing frost in fall) lasts for 171 days. As one goes west the precipitation drops off slightly, then dramatically; the growing season becomes shorter. Iowa City, Iowa, for example, records 34 inches (86.36 cm) of precipitation and has a growing season of 165 days; Scottsbluff, in western Nebraska, however, receives only 16 inches (40.64 cm) of precipitation, and the growing season there lasts for only 138 days.

In a land area so vast there are obviously great climatic differences. At International Falls, Minnesota, the July average temperature is 67°F.; during January the average temperature dips to a chilling 3°F. The growing season lasts only 107 days. At Poplar Bluff, Missouri, on the other hand, the July average temperature is 80°F., the January average temperature is 36°F., and the growing season lasts 191 days.

From year to year and decade to decade weather conditions vary. Drought and flood are not strangers to the American Heartland. But farmers and city dwellers alike have adapted to the heat of the summer and the cold, ice, and snow of the winter.

NATURAL VEGETATION
AND ANIMAL LIFE

Moderately wet Ohio, Indiana, and the southern parts of Michigan, Illinois, and Missouri were originally covered with a hardwood forest—oak, hickory, beech, and maple in the east; elm, ash, and cottonwood in the west. Much of that forest was cut down by the early settlers. West of the Wabash River, a sea of tall grass developed (the blades of *big bluestem* stood six to eight feet, or about 2 meters, high). It would be known to the early French settlers as the *prairie*. At a later date it would be covered with fields of yellow corn. And beyond the prairie, in the drier Great Plains, an area of short grass or *steppe* was destined to become the home of the great American wheat belts. In northern Michigan, northern Wisconsin, and northeastern Minnesota was the *boreal forest*, famous for the white pine which would bring the lumbermen to the western Great Lakes.

In all of the natural vegetation areas there is a rich and varied animal life. There are deer, elk, and small game in the forests of the east, bison were on the prairie and steppe, and beaver and other fur-bearing animals are in the boreal forest. In the rivers and lakes (the Great Lakes offer whitefish, lake trout and perch) there is an abundance of fish.

SOILS

The American Heartland is also marked by excellent soils. Some of the *gray-brown podzols* that developed beneath the forest cover yield fine crops. The dark brown to black *prairie soils* developed

Cattle round-up in the rugged sandstone Badlands of North Dakota

Corn flourishes in the American Heartland.
The town on the edge of this Nebraska
cornfield is over ten miles away!

under the sea of tall grass, are especially fertile. *Loess* (compacted wind-blown dust), found in the Mississippi drainage and beyond, is also very fertile and tillable.

MINERALS AND WATER

In the American Heartland can be found deposits of mineral resources—copper, lead, zinc, iron ore, limestone, and coal, among others—and an abundance of fresh water, particularly in the Great Lakes.

☆2☆

WHITE SETTLERS WEST

Before white settlers came to the American Heartland, Indians occupied the area. Shawnee, Erie and Miami, Potawatomie, Wyandot, and Lenni-Lenape were in the eastern forest; the Illinois, Iowa, Omaha, Oto, and Kansa lived on the prairie; the Pawnee, Ponca, Arikara, Mandan, and Hidatsa inhabited the prairie and plains alike; the Sioux and Cheyenne were on the plains; and the Ottawa, Menominee, and Chippewa lived in the boreal forest.

The tribesmen of the eastern forest were primarily hunters. They also fished the rivers and gathered roots, nuts, seeds, and berries in season. They lived in wigwams, in small villages. In nearby clearings they planted maize, squash, and beans. The prairie tribes hunted the bison, but they, too, were sometimes fishermen, gatherers, and farmers. The Pawnee, who lived in earth lodges on prairie and steppe, were fine bison hunters. They made their kills with bows and arrows. Pawnee women tended small gardens and collected wild fruits, berries, and mushrooms. The Sioux, like the other plains tribes, were tipi dwellers who moved from place to place in pursuit of the bison. In the boreal forest the Chippewa hunted the deer, moose, and wolf, trapped the beaver, gathered

Chippewa Indian women harvesting
wild rice in the
eastern woodlands of Wisconsin

wild rice, berries, and bark, tapped the sugar maples, and fished the rivers and lakes. They lived in villages, in wigwams covered with bulrush mats and bark. They traveled much by canoe in summer and used snowshoes and toboggans in winter.

The tribespeople had adjusted well to their varied environments. But they were keenly aware of the coming of the white settlers and the threat they posed to their lives.

FRENCH AND ENGLISH

The French had moved into the heart of the North American continent by way of the St. Lawrence River and the Great Lakes. Father Jacques Marquette and Louis Jolliet were already on the Mississippi River in 1673. A Christian mission was established among the Illinois Indians in 1675 and other missions followed. By 1735 a string of French settlements, Fort de Chartres, Saint Philippe, Prairie du Rocher, and Sainte Genevieve lined the Mississippi River. Meanwhile, in the Great Lakes country, the French had built a series of missions and forts, among them Sault Sainte Marie, Saint Ignace, Fort Michilimackinac, and Fort Pontchartrain. And French fur traders, with the help of the Indians, were ranging far and wide over the countryside.

From their settlements in the East the English also moved into the heart of the continent. George Croghan was on the Allegheny River in 1741. Before long his traders, carrying guns, powder, paint, wampum (beads of shells used by Indians as money), ribbon, and thread, were moving west to the Wabash and north to Lake Erie. They befriended the Shawnee, Miami, and Wyandot who became their best customers. In 1752 the Treaty of Logstown was signed between the English and a number of the Indian tribes, which gave the English permission to settle in the Ohio Valley.

The French were furious. They summoned their more numerous Indian allies for a battle for the continent. But in the so-called French and Indian War (1756-1763) the French were soundly beaten. In the Treaty of Paris which followed, France had to give up most of the land between the Appalachian Mountains and the Mississippi River and from the Gulf of Mexico to the Great Lakes. (New Orleans was retained and sold to Spain).

France's long-time Indian allies were greatly disturbed by the English takeover. The French had lived with them, learned their ways, given them food and credit when necessary. They were more than traders. They were friends. The English, on the other hand, would come to settle and stay. In 1763, therefore, the great Ottawa chieftain, Pontiac, struck back. He united the tribes—the Ottawa, Potawatomie, Wyandot, Shawnee, Miami, Kickapoo, Seneca, and Lenni-Lenape—and urged them to strike at the English forts. Pontiac's warriors captured eight of the twelve English forts in the West. He himself laid siege to Detroit. In 1764, however, the English broke the siege. And in the following year George Croghan made peace with the tribes.

THE AMERICANS

The English remained in the area north of the Ohio River until the Treaty of Paris was signed in 1783, years after the American Revolution. The Congress of the American Confederation, faced with the problem of managing the new land area, passed the Ordinance of 1784 which permitted the territory to be divided into as many as sixteen states. The Ordinance of 1785 provided for the area to be surveyed into townships. Each township would be six square miles (15.54 sq km) and would be divided into sections of 640 acres (259 ha). These would be sold at $1.00 per acre. Finally, the Ordinance of 1787 provided for the creation of the Northwest

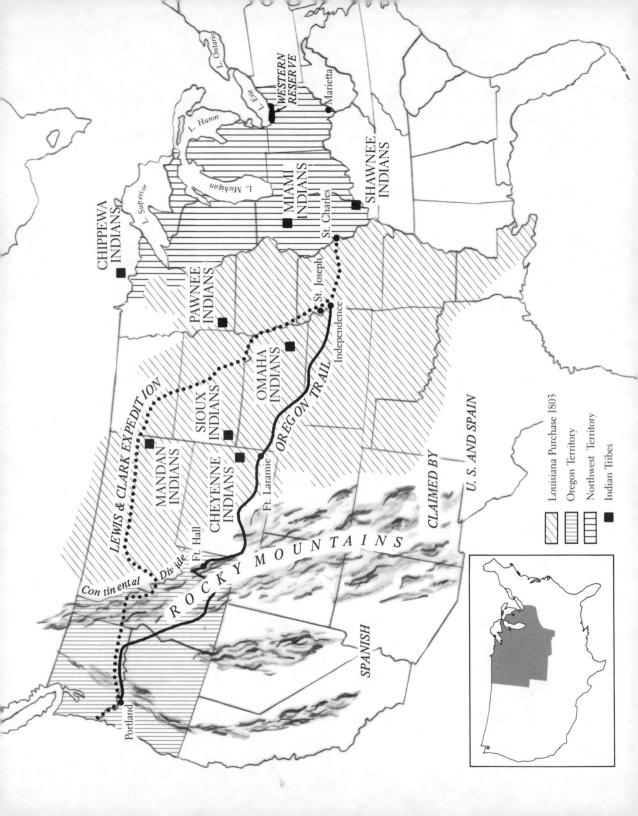

L. Ontario

L. Erie

WESTERN RESERVE

Marietta

L. Huron

SHAWNEE INDIANS

L. Superior

L. Michigan

MIAMI INDIANS

St. Charles

CHIPPEWA INDIANS

PAWNEE INDIANS

St. Joseph

Independence

LEWIS & CLARK EXPEDITION

SIOUX INDIANS

OMAHA INDIANS

OREGON TRAIL

MANDAN INDIANS

CHEYENNE INDIANS

Ft. Laramie

CLAIMED BY

U. S. AND SPAIN

Ft. Hall

Divide

R O C K Y   M O U N T A I N S

Continental

SPANISH

Portland

Louisiana Purchase 1803
Oregon Territory
Northwest Territory
Indian Tribes

Territory from which five states would be carved. A population of 60,000 would permit an application for statehood. The ordinance provided for a bill of rights and prohibited slavery north of the Ohio River.

But individuals found that the cost of land in the new Northwest Territory was too high. Only businesses could afford to buy large tracts of land, sell it, and earn a profit. So, a number of companies were formed to buy and sell land—among them the Ohio Company of Associates and the Scioto Company. The Ohio Company of Associates was made up of a group of New Englanders. They purchased 750,000 acres (303,525 ha) just west of the Seven Ranges. In 1788 the company laid out the town of Marietta (near the protection of Fort Harmar) on the left bank of the Muskingum River where it spills into the Ohio River. Land for a church, a school, and a town common was reserved. So were three-acre lots for the leading shareholders. Land was also granted for a gristmill and windmill. The building of log cabins was begun almost at once. By 1810 Marietta could boast of nearly 200 houses.

French settlers were urged to move to the Northwest Territory by the Scioto Company. Some 500 French settlers did take advantage of the opportunity. They landed in Alexandria, Virginia in fall, 1790, only to discover that the lands they had purchased were really in the tract owned by the Ohio Company of Associates. But a number did move to the area. They paid for the new acreage and built a little village—two double rows of log cabins—which they called Gallipolis. Fifty houses stood there in 1807.

The Symmes Patent or the Miami Purchase was also a business venture. Judge John Cleves Symmes and his New Jersey backers purchased 600,000 acres (242,820 ha) between the Miami and Little Miami rivers. In 1788 they laid out one settlement near the mouth of the Little Miami and another several miles below. A third settlement was built in 1789. At the same time the military

A painting of Marietta, one of
the earliest settlements in Ohio

selected a site for a new fort—Fort Washington—between the mouths of the Miami and Little Miami rivers. The settlement which grew up in the shadow of the fort would first be called Columbia and then Cincinnati. The little river village would become, of course, a major town. It had nearly 1,000 people in 1805.

There was always the threat of the Indians, however. Supported by the English, who still occupied many of their old forts, the growing American settlements were often attacked by the Indians. They turned and ran. Poorly trained American militiamen could do little against them. In 1790, an American army under General Josiah Harmar was cut to pieces near the Maumee River by Miami, Shawnee, and Kickapoo warriors. The following year, Governor Arthur St. Clair's even larger army was sent into shocking retreat with heavy American losses.

Weary of the defeats, President George Washington sent General Anthony Wayne into the Northwest Territory in 1793. Wayne trained and disciplined his troops. When the Indians attacked in 1794, Wayne stood his ground. Several months later, at Fallen Timbers, Wayne delivered a knockout blow against the tribes.

THE TREATY OF GREENVILLE

The Shawnee, Miami, Lenni-Lenape, Wyandot, Chippewa, Ottawa, and Kickapoo were at long last ready for peace. The Treaty of Greenville was signed on August 3, 1795 and ratified by the Senate on December 22nd. One of its provisions called for a boundary line separating the Indian lands from those that could be occupied by American settlers. Israel Ludlow, a veteran surveyor, began the survey of the Greenville Treaty Boundary Line in summer, 1797. His work was not completed until 1800.

The Treaty of Greenville helped to open up the western lands and led to the withdrawal of the English from their frontier posts. When the Land Act of 1800 was passed (320 acres [129.50 ha] could be purchased at $2.00 per acre and paid for over a five-year period) settlers eager for cheap land and freedom were encouraged to move west. In April, 1801 land in sections and half sections was already being sold to would-be settlers at the Cincinnati Land Office. The land rush was on.

SETTLERS WEST

Settlers often converged on the Ohio River in spring for the passage downstream. They traveled in family boats. The trip from the forks of the Ohio River to Cincinnati might take as long as two weeks, often longer. Keelboats, normally used to carry freight, were also pressed into service. So was the steamboat. The first of the steamboats, the *New Orleans*, was launched on the river in 1811. Another was built in 1814. And the numbers continued to grow. By 1819 thirty-four steamboats were built on the Ohio River. They were often packed with 50-200 settlers bound for the New West.

Movement to the Western Reserve (the land given up by the State of Connecticut in northeastern Ohio), on the other hand, was more often overland. A favorite route led from Connecticut to the Hudson and Mohawk valleys, on to Buffalo, and then along the south shore of Lake Erie to the Western Reserve. This was the approximate route followed by the original survey party under Moses Cleaveland in 1796.

The Western Reserve was laid out in five mile square (12.95 sq km) townships rather than the traditional six mile square (15.54 sq km) townships. Thousands of New Englanders flocked to the area. They set up compact agricultural settlements around the village green. School, church, burial ground, and home lots fronted the green. Beyond were the fields and the common pasture land. The Western Reserve was a bit of New England transferred to the west. This settlement pattern can still be seen today in the town of Hudson and in a number of communities in northeastern Ohio.

Early settlers moved into southern Indiana and southern Illinois via the Ohio River; they moved into southeastern Michigan via the Great Lakes. But growth in Michigan was slow. A land office opened in Detroit in 1818 apparently helped little with population growth. In 1820 the Land Sales Act (a half quarter section could be purchased at $1.25 per acre [.4047 ha]) did help to spur settlement. So did the completion of the Erie Canal in 1825 and the building of a wagon road in 1827 across the infamous Black Swamp in northern Ohio. Michigan's population increased. Roads were extended from Detroit to Chicago in 1833, and then to Port Huron, Saginaw, and Bay City. Settlers began to move into Michigan's interior.

Meanwhile American settlement had moved even farther west. In southwestern Wisconsin and neighboring Illinois and Iowa the chief attraction was the Galena dolomite—a lead ore. The galena deposits had been known for many years. Local Fox Indians had worked the lead ores on Julien Dubuque's estate on the Iowa side of the Mississippi River for decades. They had doubtlessly worked the ores on the Illinois side. But it was to the Fever River area—on the Illinois side—that American miners and settlers moved in 1819. They founded La Pointe, later called Galena, which was to become the gateway to the entire lead mining region, and its chief supply and shipping center. So great was the call for lead (for paint, pipes, sheeting, and printer's type) and so crowded were conditions in Galena that lead mining spread into neighboring Wisconsin.

The earliest Wisconsin settlements were at Hardscrabble (later called Hazel Green) and New Diggings. Rich lead ores were also discovered at Shullsburg, Platteville, Mineral Point, and Dodgeville where small villages were laid out. By 1828 there were 10,000 people in the Lead Region.

Many of the early settlers had come up from the South via the Mississippi River. But as the area grew, more migrants were attracted from the East and from abroad. "Cousin Jacks" from the mines in Cornwall, England began to arrive in 1827. By the 1830s they made up 20 percent of the Lead Region's population.

A good many miners in the Lead Region also devoted their talents part-time to agriculture. On the prairie or in the neighboring uplands of the Driftless Area they raised grain and vegetables. And while people were settling in the Lead Region, other settlers, following the Black Hawk War (1832), were beginning to occupy southeastern Wisconsin.

Americans were also beginning to push into Iowa. They came after the Sac and Fox Indians had ceded a fifty-mile (80.46 km) strip of land along the Mississippi River to the United States in 1833. They came as squatters and organized "claim clubs" to protect their interests. By 1836 there were 10,000 Americans in Iowa. In 1838 the government opened land offices in the newly created Iowa Territory.

Minnesota, too, was beginning to attract American settlers. Fort Snelling, at the mouth of the Minnesota River, signalled the American presence in 1819. The newly arrived founded Mankato near the edge of the prairie and then moved into the Big Woods between the Minnesota and Mississippi rivers. Settlement lagged in much of the north and west because the area was the home of the Sioux and Chippewa Indians, mortal enemies who did not wish their land intruded upon. But there were those who were prepared to pounce upon the Indian lands when title to them was secured.

Farther south in Missouri, the old French settlements had long been in place. In 1764, just below the junction of the Missouri and Mississippi rivers, Pierre Laclede and Auguste Chouteau—fresh from New Orleans—had laid out a small village. It was called Laclede's Village but would soon be known as St. Louis. Indians and French-Canadian trappers visited the site. St. Louis became an important trading center. At the time of the Louisiana Purchase (the United States purchased Louisiana from France for $15,000,000 in 1803) St. Louis' population was over 1,000. In 1807 the village had 200 houses. In 1821 the first state legislature met in St. Louis' Missouri Hotel. City status was achieved in 1823.

The Louisiana Purchase, of course, sent Americans even farther west. Meriwether Lewis and William Clark, on a government expedition from 1804 to 1806, passed from prairie to steppe while exploring the American West. They moved up the Missouri River, stopped at the Mandan Indian villages, crossed the Rocky Mountains, and went on to the Pacific coast and then returned. They had discovered an important route to the Pacific Ocean. In 1806, Captain Zebulon M. Pike visited the Osage and Pawnee Indian villages and continued west on the Arkansas River. Captured by the Spaniards, he was taken prisoner to Mexico, but was later released. Major Stephen H. Long, another western traveler, knew the prairie and the dry plains better than most. He may have been responsible for giving the Great American Desert, which covers much of the prairie and steppe land of the West, its name.

The Great American Desert was certainly no place for American agriculture. Perhaps America's settlement had reached its limits in Iowa and Missouri. What American settler in search of a good piece of well-watered land would risk moving to the western steppe country? The western prairie and steppe were, therefore, shunned by settlers. Yet Kansas and Nebraska became important roadways to the west. Travelers on the Santa Fe Trail, for exam-

ple, left Independence or Franklin, Missouri and moved west to Council Grove in Kansas, near the edge of the High Plains, where they rested their mules and oxen. From Council Grove they moved on to Pawnee Rock at the great bend of the Arkansas River and followed the left bank of the river into Colorado before moving south to Santa Fe. Some traders left the Arkansas River near present-day Dodge City, Kansas, and traveled south over the grass-poor and practically waterless Cimarron Crossing. William Becknell, the "Father of the Santa Fe Trail," made one trip in 1821 and another in 1822. Between 1830 and 1840 traders made their trips under military escort. The Indian threat was still very great.

Settlers bound for Oregon also crossed prairie and steppe. Pioneer families gathered at Independence, St. Joseph, or Council Bluffs and moved west across Nebraska by way of the Platte River. They then journeyed west through South Pass to Fort Hall and on to Oregon by way of the Snake and Columbia rivers. The wheels of the wagons made deep ruts in the Kansas and Nebraska earth. Traces can still be seen.

Before long settlers even began to move into the dry country of Kansas, Nebraska, and the Dakotas. Speculators, people interested in making profits in land, tried to draw residents to prairie and steppe. In the 1840s they laid out imaginary towns in an effort to encourage settlers west. They advertised in newspapers, built hotels in their would-be communities, and offered to give lots

Lewis and Clark stop at a Mandan Indian village along the Missouri River during their exploration of territory gained by the Louisiana Purchase.

away. How could one resist the temptations of Omaha City, Kearney City, Emporia, or Eureka?

Actually Leavenworth became the first town in Kansas. It was formed by a group of Missourians in June, 1854. Atchison was formed in July, Lawrence in August, and Topeka in December. In the summer of 1854 Lawrence was a village of tents. One year later most of the houses were made of sod—with some frame support. Brownsville, Nebraska was laid out in 1855, Beatrice in 1857. The Western Town Company and the Dakota Land Company founded Sioux Falls City in 1857 and by 1858 settlers were moving into eastern Dakota.

Meanwhile, behind the growing sod house frontier a relatively "civilized" nation was emerging. And in the vast area between Ohio and Nebraska an American Heartland was evolving.

A Nebraska family in front
of their prairie sod house

THE DEVELOPMENT OF AGRICULTURE

Settlers arriving in southern Ohio early in the nineteenth century came with little more than a few sticks of furniture, a rifle, a hog or two, some corn, and the seeds of squash or other vegetables. On their new acres they went immediately to work. The first tasks were to clear the trees, build a cabin, turn the soil, and make the first plantings. These were difficult tasks indeed. Fortunately, food was not a pressing problem. The forest provided game—deer, bear, turkey, squirrel, and raccoon in addition to nuts, seeds, and wild berries. The newly arrived settlers could eat their fill while the work went on.

In the fine Ohio soil the early settlers planted corn and wheat. They raised hemp and flax, barley, oats, and rye. They planted fruit trees—apples, cherries, peaches, pears, and plums—and vegetable gardens. In March, after the snows of winter had disappeared, a settler-farmer might sow turnip and pea seeds, then parsley, pepper, and cauliflower. He might plant potatoes and cabbages. When the frost was out of the ground in late April he might sow lima and bush beans. By mid-June he was already making his first harvests.

In the earliest years the settler-farmers made their plantings simply to satisfy their own needs. Before long, however, they began to send their produce to market. Some farmers raised flocks of sheep, others beef cattle and dairy cows. The beef cattle were fattened on the Ohio farms for the eastern markets of Philadelphia and Baltimore. By 1815 flatboats, keelboats, and steamboats were carrying meat and produce to the lower Ohio and Mississippi River communities.

Despite the weather conditions, an occasional drought, the crude farm tools, the weeds, the Hessian flies and greenworms, and the squirrels, mice, wolves, and wildcats, agriculture prospered. Visitors and travelers noted the new frame houses with brick chimneys and glass windowpanes, the wells, stables, corn cribs, and outbuildings; the farmland divided into fields enclosed by rail fences; and the thriving apple and peach orchards.

AMERICAN CORN BELT

By 1820 a system of agriculture had evolved north of the Ohio River that would remain for over one hundred years, and that would lead to the creation of the American Corn Belt. That system was based upon a three-year rotation of crops (corn, small grains, and hay) and the feeding of these crops to hogs and cattle. The cheap, hardy, and high-yielding corn plant was the kingpin of the rotation. The soils north of the Ohio River were ideal for the corn plant. So, too, were the long growing season, the hot days and nights of July and August, and the summer rainfall. The corn plant thrived.

Next in the rotation were the small grains: winter wheat in the southern part of the area, oats in the northern portions. Winter wheat served the rotation well. Because it grew faster, it offered protection from the sun and rain to the slower growing hay crops whose seeds were planted at the same time. Winter wheat was in constant demand, could be shipped over long distances to market without fear of spoilage, and brought a good price. Oats were used as a feed for horses and with corn for cattle and sheep. The hay crops (clover and alfalfa), of course, completed the rotation.

Corn growing—and with it the raising of hogs—increased quite rapidly. The emerging Corn Belt was moving west into the true prairie country.

THE TRUE PRAIRIE

Settlers had shunned the true prairie for years. They had found it difficult to cope with the thick root structure of the bluestem grass. The cast iron plows used in the east were of little use on the prairie. Even with John Deere's improved steel plow, settlers did not rush to the prairie. There were many other problems. The prairie lacked timber so important for home building, fence making, and fuel. Much of the land was flat and poorly drained. And poor drainage was often cited as a reason for illness.

Those who did move to the prairie settled close to the rivers, near wooded areas, or on the land close to the prairie edge. It was left for the railroads and private speculators in land to open the prairie country for settlement.

In the 1850s a dense network of rails was built across Illinois, connecting with lines in Iowa and Missouri. The railroad companies—the Illinois Central among them—had been granted mortgages (title to property, but title is lost if proper payment is not made) by the government. They could repay the mortgages by selling the land to potential settlers. As a result the railroads issued hundreds of thousands of pamphlets and brochures pointing out the beauties and virtues of the prairie earth. At the very same time land speculators also issued guidebooks and brochures urging settlers to make their homes on the prairie.

—34—

The prairie was not inviting
to early settlers, and isolated houses
like this one were typical.

Hundreds of thousands of people flocked to the prairie earth. Some bought their own acres. Others, finding the price of land too high, went to work as tenant farmers for the new land speculators. Before long a corn-cattle-hog economy was beginning to mature.

Following the Civil War, homesteaders moved in increasing numbers to Kansas and Nebraska. Farmers from the emerging Corn Belt were moving west from the relatively wet bluestem prairie into the much drier buffalo and grama grass steppe. They brought their corn with them and after breaking the ground planted it in the new earth. They raised wheat and oats. They built sod houses, fences, and barns for horses and livestock. They began to set their roots in the new earth.

In 1874 came calamity. Grasshoppers, by the hundreds of thousands—perhaps millions—carried by the wind, fell like a storm on the plains. The sun was hidden. Grasshoppers were everywhere. They devoured everything edible in their path. They gnawed into the farm tools; they ate the horse harnesses in the barns; they stopped the trains from running across Kansas and Nebraska. And they came again and again, in 1875, 1876, and 1877.

There were other hazards too—prairie fires and drought, storms and floods, and devastating blizzards. The faint-hearted left

This old drawing shows a train crossing the Nebraska plains being brought to a complete halt by masses of grasshoppers that obliterated the railroad tracks. Swarms of grasshoppers plagued the prairie for four years (1874–1877) and then, mysteriously, were never seen again.

the short grass country. Those who remained received aid from relatives and government alike. But they had to change their farming practices.

WINTER WHEAT AND SPRING WHEAT BELTS

They tried different kinds of crops. They experimented with corn. They planted winter wheat in abundance. Planted in early autumn and harvested in late June and early July, the winter wheat crop survived the ravages of grasshoppers and other hazards. The crop was taken from the earth before the grasshoppers arrived. Thus more and more winter wheat was planted in central and western Kansas. The newly arrived Mennonites from South Russia introduced a special variety—Turkey Red—that did well in the Kansas earth. Because water was scarce the farmers permitted the fields to lie fallow (unused) every other year so that the rains of two years could be used for growing a single crop.

Thus a Winter Wheat Belt was born in the center of the North American continent. By early in the twentieth century it extended from central Oklahoma, through Kansas, into southern Nebraska. Farther north a Spring Wheat Belt also came into existence. It stretched from the Dakotas and western Minnesota into the Prairie Provinces of Canada.

MECHANIZATION

The thrusts into the wheat country were made possible in part by the introduction of new farm machinery. A reaper had been patented in 1811 and Cyrus McCormick had patented his in 1834. But the old cutting tools—the sickle and scythe—continued to be used for cutting grain. In 1849 the McCormick plant in Chicago manufactured only 1,500 reapers. In 1874 the same plant built 10,000 and in 1884, the year of McCormick's death, 80,000. Farmers were becoming more and more interested in the work the reaper could perform. They also discovered that the Marsh harvester, invented by C.W. and W.W. Marsh in 1858, helped to speed the harvesting process, and that binding the grain was made simpler by the mechanical knotter and John F. Appleby's twine binder of 1878. New threshing machines and seeders were developed.

But the mechanization of agriculture was hardly complete. The twentieth century witnessed the arrival of the tractor in 1905 and the combine, which reaps, threshes, and bags grain automatically. The "baby combine" of 1936 could even be used on the small family farm.

The new machinery lightened the farmer's work load. It made possible the "bonanza farms" of the Red River Valley in Minnesota and North Dakota and the greater west, and it helped to increase considerably the farmer's production.

NORTH CENTRAL
DAIRY REGION

Farther east in Wisconsin the agricultural pattern had evolved somewhat differently. Machines and expanding settlement had helped increase the planting of winter wheat. But the light soils could not handle the excessive drain of nitrogen. Yields per acre began to decline. In 1860 the state had had a banner production year—29,000,000 bushels; in the following years, however, production decreased even when more land was occupied in the north and west. And there were other problems. The wheat crops were plagued by the chinch bug and plant diseases; the farmers were hit hard by rising costs and taxes. A choice had to be made—either abandon the Wisconsin acres or, like the western Kansas and Nebraska farmers, change the farming practices.

*A turn-of-the-century
harvest scene in Kansas*

Wisconsin's farmers began, therefore, to raise sheep, hogs, or beef cattle. They planted corn, hay, and oats. Finally, they turned to the dairy cow.

Daniel D. Hoard, editor of *Hoard's Dairyman*, urged Wisconsin farmers to concentrate on milk and milk products—and therefore dairy cows. Jerseys, Holsteins, and later Guernseys were brought in to stock Wisconsin's herds. By the turn of the twentieth century milk cows were to be found on 90 percent of Wisconsin's farms. Meanwhile, farmers had turned to alfalfa to restore nitrogen to the soil. They had built their first silo for storing feed in 1877. The silo was to become an important part of the Wisconsin landscape.

In the push toward dairying Wisconsin became a leading butter- and cheese-producing state. Cheddar and Colby (a variety of Cheddar) became almost instant favorites. They were shipped by train via Chicago to New York and were even sold in London. After the turn of the twentieth century the marketing of dried, condensed, and pasteurized milk became increasingly significant.

While any number of Wisconsin's farmers turned to raising corn and hogs, to grain and cattle, or to hops for making beer, in later years, the dairying persisted. A North Central Dairy Region was created. And Wisconsin still calls itself America's Dairyland.

VALUES IN THE AMERICAN HEARTLAND

The New Englanders, other Americans, and immigrants from Europe who found their way to the American Heartland had to adapt to their new environment. A set of distinctive traits came to characterize the people who settled in this region.

For the farmer-settler, for example, hard work was a virtue. Farmers often toiled from dawn until dusk. Many farmers—especially dairy farmers—worked seven days a week with little or no rest. There was a general feeling that anyone who worked hard would certainly prosper. The family was all-important, the kingpin of the American Heartland value system.

The farmers of the American Heartland were efficient and progressive. They adopted the new machinery and later adapted to the use of fertilizers and pesticides. They helped to build a number of America's great universities dedicated to agriculture, science, and practical and applied knowledge.

Much of the population was essentially conservative in politics. Many joined and supported the Republican Party, for it upheld the capitalistic system and governed with a minimum of interference.

CHANGES IN THE AMERICAN HEARTLAND

Great changes came to the American Heartland, and farmers were called upon to give their best in good times and in bad.

One change involved the soybean. The shallow-rooted legume, imported from China, was adopted for the crop rotation. It replaced the small grains and hay and served the farmer as feed. During World War II, when the need for soybean oil and high protein meal increased, the farmers planted more and more of it. By the 1970s the soybean had become a most important crop and

Since World War II the soybean has grown in importance. Shown here is a closeup of the crop during harvest on an Iowa farm.

was part of a two-year corn-soybean rotation. Southern Illinois and northern Missouri had more acres planted in soybean than in corn. And there was talk of a newly developing Corn-Soybean Belt.

Even more remarkable was the progress made in hybrid corn. Experiments in hybridization (mating corns to produce a better corn) had been carried out early in the twentieth century. In 1933, during the Great Depression when unemployment rose to record highs, a number of Iowa farmers invested in hybrid corn seed. The crops they grew were successful. In 1939 three-fourths of Iowa's corn acreage was already in hybrid corn; during World War II that figure rose to nearly 100 percent.

Meanwhile machines had also come to the hybrid corn fields. The mechanical corn picker and ultimately the picker-sheller could pick, husk, and shell the corn—all in one operation—right from the stalk. The farmer of the American Heartland was living in, if not a new world, then certainly a different one.

MATURE AMERICAN HEARTLAND

Following the Great Depression and World War II, the now mature American Heartland entered into a time of relative prosperity. The family farm did decline, of course, as farms became larger and farmers fewer. In 1940, thirty million people lived on six

Modern machinery like the picker-sheller (right) which picks, husks, and shells the corn automatically, and the wheat harvesting combine (over) are in part responsible for the incredible yields of today's American farms.

million farms; by 1974 there were fewer than ten million people living on 2.8 million farms. And farms were vanishing at an astonishing rate—some 70 per day. But many family farms were still able to compete with the new agri-corporations, as they are called. They were able to produce better than 60 percent of the farm produce of the American Heartland.

Imagine a large modern family farm in Iowa that produced in 1974—a single year—27,000 bushels of corn, plus oats and hay, all fed to the animals! Its hog house yielded ham and bacon, tenderloin and roast, chops, ribs and sausage—enough for over 3,500 Americans. Its dairy could supply milk for 600 young people, and its cows could provide meat for 30,000 quarter-pound patties. Everything was mechanized and electrified. Imagine riding at the wheel of a new tractor in air-conditioned comfort while listening to the stereo in the cab! The old farmer-settler would have gazed in absolute wonder!

THE 1980s

These are not particularly good years for the farmers in the American Heartland. Soaring interest rates, the easy credit of the 70s, and depressed prices have caught them in a bind. The farmers have huge stocks of grain, but the prices are too low for them to make a profit. Net income per farm has dropped considerably. From Ohio to Nebraska farmers are threatened with losing their long-held family farms.

The Reagan administration, through a government program called PIK, or "payment in kind," is trying to help. PIK calls for reducing production on the farms—growing less grain, even idling the acres. Farmers will then be paid in corn for not growing corn. Under this plan it is expected that prices will go up and that any number of farms will be saved.

But the outlook is still grim. How will the conditions of the early '80s affect the American Heartland farmer? Will the strong, independent farmer be able to survive in the '90s and well into the twenty-first century?

☆**4**☆

THE GROWTH OF INDUSTRY

The urge to manufacture had early beginnings in the American Heartland. Farmer-settlers in Ohio found that goods imported from the East were often very expensive. A single item—salt— brought over the Alleghenies on packhorses might sell for $6.00 to $10.00 per bushel. And salt was a necessity. Even when supplies were brought across the river from Kentucky the price was high. The farmer-settlers, therefore, began to talk about economic independence—about making all sorts of goods locally. They concentrated first on salt-making.

There were saltwater deposits near Zanesville, in the Great Kanawha Valley across the Ohio River, and near Shawneetown, Illinois—the so-called Wabash Salines. The "mining" and "manufacturing" processes were quite similar. Wells were dug and lined with the wood of the gum tree; deep wells were encased in metal. The saltwater was forced to the surface and into large kettles by pump. Heat applied by burning wood and, after 1817, by coal in "furnaces" helped in the evaporation process. At the Wabash Salines about one hundred and twenty gallons of water yielded sixty pounds of salt. In 1828 it was selling from between 37½¢ to 50¢ per bushel—the price had come down markedly—and was a common item in the Ohio River trade.

There were also advantages to building many other things locally—among them gristmills and sawmills. The earlier mills—handmills similar to those of the Indians—had proven less than efficient. In the new gristmill, grain could easily be converted into flour and prepared for local use or export. In the new sawmill, lumber could be cut for local houses, barns, and boats; it could also be prepared for eventual sale, perhaps downriver.

The early manufacturers soon began to use their corn and rye to make whiskey. They brewed beer and ale and sold it in the river communities. They made maple sugar. They tanned leather, made grindstones, and even manufactured paper for newsprint. Women were encouraged to make their own household products and garments. They worked on spinning wheels and looms and turned out fine woolen goods and linens. They made rope from home-grown hemp.

As the small towns grew, there was a tendency for the factories to be established within their boundaries. Cincinnati, for example, had a population of 2,320 in 1810; by 1830 it had reached 30,000. It was truly the metropolis of the western country. Its early manufactured products included cotton spinning, and pottery, glass, paint, and saddle making. By 1826 Cincinnati was sending numerous factory-made products into the export market (flour, varieties of pork, whiskey, feathers, hats, clothing, and furniture) and was receiving in return bar iron, liquors, dry goods, tea, and

Cincinnati, on the Ohio River, was already a leading manufacturing town by the 1830s.

—50—

coffee. In 1828 sixty steamboats were made on Cincinnati's waterfront.

Two years earlier an Ohio ironmaster had set up a charcoal furnace near Ironton. He began to make pig iron (crude iron that comes directly from a furnace.) Then John Campbell introduced the hot blast method in his furnace at nearby Hanging Rock. When yields began to increase, other iron workers were attracted to the area. Before long they were preparing hammers, cooking utensils, shoe lasts, and other items of iron. Fine iron deposits, handsome stands of timber, plentiful limestone, and a never-ending supply of water continued to lure the ironmasters. During the 1830s and 1840s many new furnaces were built in southern Ohio and neighboring Kentucky—the Hanging Rock Iron District. And for a thirty-five year period this area was the leading iron-producing region in the United States.

West and north of Ohio, in the years before the Civil War, settlers were producing an array of manufactured goods: lumber, flour, clothing, boots and shoes, barrels, staves and hoops, shingles, sashes, doors and furniture, saddles and harnesses, carts and wagons, and as one might suspect, agricultural implements. Cyrus McCormick of Chicago was building and selling his reaper. Jerome I. Case of Racine, Wisconsin was making his thresher. In Milwaukee master workers were brewing beer, making flour, and manufacturing a wide variety of lumber products.

Out on the plains of Kansas, Nebraska, and the Dakotas the early manufactured products were quite similar to those made farther east. Salt, as we have seen, was an important item. So were gristmills and sawmills. Important, too, was the manufacture of flour and lumber, liquor, boots and shoes, carriages, carts and wagons, soap, candles, and stoneware. There were also a few exotics: cigar and tobacco manufacturing plants in Brownville, Nebraska, Nebraska City, and Yankton, South Dakota; a silk factory in eastern Kansas; a cotton gin; a plant that made castor oil; and a gypsum mill making plaster of Paris. In the 1880s there were firms in Kansas and Nebraska making windmills and barbed wire.

The emerging American Heartland would build successfully on the old "frontier" industries; but it would rise to power on the broad shoulders of iron and steel, and after the turn of the century, on the vigor of the new automobile. Both industries would depend largely on the raw materials of the Great Lakes area and on the incomparable Great Lakes waterway itself. Both would depend on the latest techniques in planning, management, and technology. Both would depend on the energy and skill of the American worker. Both would help to drastically change American life. And both—together with agriculture—would help to create the American Heartland.

THE RISE OF THE IRON AND STEEL INDUSTRY

On September 19, 1844 William A. Burt, Michigan's master surveyor, was shocked by the fluctuations of his magnetic compass needle. Never before had the little needle behaved so. But the reason soon became evident. Burt had discovered, just south of present-day Negaunee, Michigan, the rich iron ores of the Lake Superior District.

A number of companies were quickly formed to mine the ores. Hand drills, picks, sledge hammers, and black powder were used to break up the rocks bearing the iron. The companies brought in their own forges to make "bloom iron" on the spot. Negaunee even had a blast furnace in 1858, and others were built in a number of other places in the Upper Peninsula of Michigan. But most of the ore was not fed to the local furnaces; it was shipped instead to the ports on the lower Great Lakes and east to Pittsburgh.

Unfortunately there was a great bottleneck along the way.

Lake Superior stands some twenty-one feet (6.4 m) above the level of Lakes Michigan and Huron. The St. Marys River, which connects the water bodies, flows swiftly, therefore, and is rapid-filled. The local Chippewa Indians navigated the river only with difficulty. How would the iron companies ship their ores around the bottleneck? One solution often used was a tramway built around the rapids over which carts and wagons carrying the ore could move. Another solution was the use of greased rollers on which even large boats could be pulled or towed. The *Independence* and the *Julia Palmer*, for example, two steam-powered vessels, were transported from Lake Michigan to Lake Superior in 1845 and again in 1846. With increased cargoes of ore and other materials approaching the bottleneck a new solution was necessary—a canal.

The St. Marys Falls Ship Canal Company went to work in the summer of 1853. Tools, supplies, horses, and workers were brought together at Sault Sainte Marie. The blasting could be heard well into the long summer evenings. In winter, work was stopped by the often blizzard-like conditions. Still, the building went on. On May 31, 1855 the lock canal at the "Soo" was completed; on June 18 the first ships passed through the locks.

THE SHIFT IN STEELMAKING

Pittsburgh, Pennsylvania, had risen to a most important position in the steel industry. It was sitting on the soft coal fields of western Pennsylvania. It was near the Connellsville coke, so important in the making of steel. It had local supplies of limestone that was

A freighter passing through one of the present-day "Soo" locks

needed in her furnaces. It was also blessed with good local iron ores. And it was located on a fine waterway and had excellent rail connections with both east and west. But Pittsburgh's continued growth depended in large measure on the iron ores from the Lake Superior District.

So great was Pittsburgh's success that there was a spillover into the neighboring Pennsylvania communities and on into West Virginia (Weirton and Wheeling), Ohio (Youngstown, Steubenville, and Canton-Massilon) and into the older Hanging Rock Iron District. And more and more manufacturers were moving to locations on the Great Lakes. There they could unload their cargoes right alongside the blast furnaces. It would cost them less money. In 1900 Lackawanna Steel Company showed the way. They moved their plant from Scranton, Pennsylvania to Buffalo, New York, on Lake Erie. And other companies erected their furnaces in Cleveland, Lorain, Sandusky, Toledo, and Detroit.

Meanwhile the iron industry had opened up new ground in the Lake Superior District. They were on the Menominee Range in 1877, the Vermilion and Gogebic ranges in 1884, and on the great Mesabi Range in 1892. And the American Heartland was being called upon for more and more of its wealth.

When the United States Steel Corporation was making plans for its new steel plant in 1907 a Great Lakes site was decided upon. The planners realized that they could bring in iron ore from the Lake Superior District by water, and therefore at low cost. The limestone could be assembled from the quarries on the western shore of Lake Huron. The coal could be brought in from Illinois

Nineteenth-century iron miners
in Minnesota's rich Mesabi Range

after a short rail haul. It, too, would be relatively cheap. At the same time the new plant would be located in a teeming market. They could sell their products with ease. They built their plant on the Indiana dunes, facing Lake Michigan. They called the new place Gary.

Gary prospered. And so did the United States iron and steel industry. But iron and steel—like the country—has had its share of difficult times. The year 1921 was one such time. Another was the Great Depression of the 1930s. The industry has known boom and near collapse. In 1916, for example, a World War I year, 64,000,000 tons of iron ore passed through the Soo locks; in 1921— the lean year—only 25,000,000 tons made the passage. Over 64,000,000 tons of raw steel were produced in the United States in 1916; but fewer than 22,000,000 tons in 1921.

Yet more and more of the raw steel was being made in the Great Lakes region as opposed to other regions in the country. In 1904 the Great Lakes region produced but 16.1 percent of the raw steel made in the United States; by 1929 the figure was already 23.2 percent and rising. A good part of the increase was due to the coming of that new little machine—the automobile.

THE COMING
OF THE AUTOMOBILE

The bicycle had shown the way. For the "wheels" as they were called, had produced the need for the pneumatic tire and the hard surface road—both vital in the development of the automobile. Fine over short distances, bicycle travel was terribly wearying over long distances. A new vehicle was needed—a mechanically driven one that could move with ease over a hard surface road, one that could move swiftly and safely.

In both Europe and America attempts were made to make such a vehicle. Charles E. Duryea and his brother Frank (they were bicycle mechanics) built a motor carriage, with a one-cylinder gasoline engine, that they operated on the streets of Springfield, Massachusetts in 1893. Elwood Haynes and his partners, working in Kokomo, Indiana, made a similar vehicle in 1894. In 1896 Ransom E. Olds of Lansing, Michigan built and displayed his single-cylinder, five-horsepower "horseless carriage."

Olds had arrived in Lansing from Ohio in 1880. As a young man he worked in his father's machine shop as a machinist and bookkeeper. In 1887 Olds built his first horseless carriage—a steam vehicle. A three-wheeler, the steamer weighed 1,500 pounds (680.40 kg) and could run—at times—up to ten miles (16 km) per hour. Olds tinkered and experimented. In 1891 he produced a new model. But he was not quite satisfied with the steamer. Having heard about the work of the Germans on the gasoline engine Olds turned to it. In 1896 his horseless carriage, powered by an internal combustion engine, was completed. But Olds was hardly satisfied. He continued to build other models. He wanted to build an automobile that was cheap, durable, and easy to operate. In 1900, in his new Detroit plant, he built and tested the "curved dash runabout," the first car to carry the name Oldsmobile. In 1901 Olds made 425 runabouts; 5,508 were made in 1904. The automobile was beginning to make an impact on America.

Henry Ford was also an early automotive "inventor." He had built his first car, a one-seater with a two-cylinder engine, in 1896. It was not a huge success. In 1903 he organized the Ford Motor Company and continued to experiment. Then came other models, including in 1908, the famous Model T, the "flivver," or "tin lizzie."

The new model was made of alloy steels, was served by a four-cylinder engine, had two speeds forward and one in reverse, and could be operated with foot pedals. It was painted a sober black. But it was not quite cheap enough. For a number of years, therefore, Ford and his employees worked on cutting the costs of

manufacture. They standardized the parts—wheels, axles, engines, nuts, and bolts were all made alike. Each would fit any machine of the same model. They added a moving assembly line. They began to mass produce the Model T. In 1913 they introduced a conveyor belt system for assembling parts and a similar system for building the car bodies. With these innovations they were able to cut the time of manufacture and therefore the costs to the consumer.

In 1908, 5,986 Model T's were built; each sold for $850.00. By 1916 well over 500,000 cars were built; each sold for only $360.00. Ford had helped to create a revolution. He had brought the possibility of owning an automobile to nearly every American.

Ford had also helped establish the American automobile industry in the Detroit area—in Michigan—in a portion of the emerging American Heartland. General Motors and Chrysler also chose to build their empires in Detroit. So big did the automobile industry become in Detroit, that like steel in Pittsburgh, it simply spilled over. Flint, Pontiac, Lansing, and Jackson (Michigan) all became automobile towns. And automobile manufacturing became tremendously important in Ohio (Cleveland and Toledo), Indiana (South Bend and Indianapolis), Wisconsin (Kenosha) and Illinois (Chicago).

But like the iron and steel industry, the automobile industry followed the "boom and bust" pattern. Fewer than 2,000,000 new cars were made in 1921; over 5,000,000 in 1929. There was a dip during the Great Depression. Fewer than 1,000,000 cars were produced during each of the World War II years, but over 5,000,000 were produced in 1948.

Model T chassis are driven into position for final assembly at a Ford plant in Michigan in 1914.

TACONITE

With World War II came still another problem—a growing realization that the iron resources of the Lake Superior District were fast giving out. Millions upon millions of tons of ore had been taken from the Iron Ranges. The high grade ores—like those on Mesabi—could not last forever.

In Minnesota, therefore, the industrialists turned to the low-grade ores—the taconites—in an effort to save the iron-producing area. They used "jet piercers" to drill into the hard taconite. They had to learn to bring up the low iron content (15-45 percent) to a point (over 51 percent) where they could be used directly in the blast furnaces. They had to learn to crush, consolidate, and "agglomerate" the ores. The last by making pellets, a process developed at the Mines Experiment Station of the University of Minnesota, under the direction of E.W. Davis who is often called the "Father of the Taconite Industry." Today taconite pellets are used regularly in the blast furnaces of the Great Lakes area.

THE FOSSIL FUELS

Petroleum, natural gas, and coal are called the fossil fuels because they were derived largely from old plant and/or animal life. In the American Heartland there are producing petroleum, or oil, fields in Kansas and Nebraska, the Dakotas, Illinois, Indiana, Michigan, and Ohio. But there is not enough oil to supply the North Central states. Oil pipelines, therefore, have been built to bring oil to the American Heartland from the southwest and the oil-producing regions of Canada.

An oil refinery in Kansas

Natural gas is found in Kansas, and in smaller amounts in North Dakota, Indiana, Michigan, and Ohio. It, too, is brought to the American Heartland by pipeline from the Gulf Coast, Texas, and Canada.

Portions of the Appalachian coal fields (Ohio), the Eastern Interior coal fields (Illinois, Indiana, and Iowa), and the Western Interior coal fields (Iowa, Missouri, Kansas, and Nebraska) are all found in the American Heartland. The Eastern Interior fields contain good bituminous coal. Much of it is mined underground at depths of 1,000 feet (1,600 m). This coal is often mixed with coal from the Appalachian coal fields for use in the iron and steel mills.

CEREAL

In the 1870s Dr. John Kellogg helped to found the Battle Creek, Michigan Sanitarium (hospital). Much concerned with the diet of his patients, Dr. Kellogg turned to cereals to find foods that were tasteful and nutritious. One of the sanitarium's former patients, C.W. Post, marketed Grape Nuts before the turn of the century. And Dr. Kellogg's brother, W. K. Kellogg, began to manufacture Corn Flakes in 1899. Today, Grape Nuts, Corn Flakes, and many other cereals—made from the harvests of the American Heartland—are widely sold all over the world.

THE 1970S AND 1980S

In the 1970s there were new problems—rising gasoline prices, high interest rates, and the beginnings of high unemployment and a general recession. Some even called it a depression. In 1978 United States automobile manufacturers sold over nine million cars; In 1982 fewer than 6 million cars were sold. The experts were beginning to ask, "Why?" Was the sharp decline due to competition

*Michigan is still feeling the effects
of the slump in the auto industry.
Here the unemployed seek help
at a food stamp center.*

from the Japanese and German automakers? Was it because American labor costs were too high? Was it because our plants were too old and could no longer compete? Was it because America was changing and could no longer rely on automobiles and iron and steel as it had in the past?

For whatever the reasons, the unemployment lines grew longer in the late 1970s and early 1980s. The "Big Three" automakers (General Motors, Ford, and Chrysler) were forced to cut 250,000 jobs. They closed twenty-five plants. Michigan's unemployment rate, at times the highest in the nation, soared to a staggering 17 percent. Detroit, Flint, and Pontiac could almost be called disaster areas.

It was virtually the same in the iron and steel industry. There were plant closings and high unemployment. The future looked bleak. On September 19, 1977—Black Monday—Youngstown Sheet and Tube closed its massive plant in Campbell, just outside of Youngstown, Ohio. Four thousand, two hundred people were thrown out of work. Ten thousand were unemployed in the Mahoning Valley alone. The American Heartland was reeling.

But there is already talk of retooling, of a drive for new technology, of labor-management harmony, of sales of over 9,000,000 cars—perhaps by 1985. Is the American Heartland now preparing for a new upward surge?

☆5☆

THE CITIES

In the last quarter of the nineteenth century the face of the American Heartland began to change a great deal. People were beginning to leave the rural areas for the growing towns and cities. And their numbers were swelled by the immigrants—the Scandinavians and Germans, the Irish, the Poles and Czechs, the Polish and Russian Jews, and the Italians—coming in ever greater numbers from Europe.

By 1880 one of every five people in the American Heartland lived in a community of 4,000 or more. In 1890 it was one of every three. And Ohio and Illinois could boast of one hundred and twenty towns and cities. In Minnesota and Missouri three of every ten people were already townsfolk.

The growth of the cities was often incredible. Chicago was a big city in 1880; it had over 500,000 people. But it had over 1,000,000 people in 1890 and was the second largest city in the country. Detroit, Milwaukee, Cleveland, and Columbus increased in size between 60 percent and 80 percent during the same period. Minneapolis-St. Paul tripled in size. Of the fifty largest cities in the United States in 1890, twelve were located in the American Heartland. All were growing; all were maturing; all were changing.

CHICAGO

Fort Dearborn had been laid out on the Chicago site in 1803. But the town itself was not formally plotted until 1830. Because of its location on Lake Michigan and its control of routes into the interior, the little town grew quickly. By 1837, when it was incorporated as a city, Chicago already had over 4,000 people. Lumbering and meat packing were its leading industries.

A great spur to the city's growth was the building of the rail lines. By 1856 Chicago was served by ten trunk lines that had about 3,000 miles (4830 km) of track. Fifty-eight passenger trains and thirty-eight freight trains entered and left the city each day. Chicago would become the largest railroad center in the world. The city also became a center of the grain trade. Grain elevators dominated the skyline. In 1865 the Union Stock Yards were completed and the first steel rails were made in the city. Cyrus McCormick built his new plant on the Chicago River. He was soon turning out as many as 10,000 reapers a year.

Chicago was a great success. It had nearly 300,000 people in 1870. The future looked bright indeed. But in October of the following year the Great Chicago Fire destroyed practically every building in the downtown area. The fire left 300 dead, 90,000 homeless, and property losses at a staggering $200,000,000.

The fire did not defeat the city. Chicago rebuilt in brick and iron. Skyscrapers were added to the skyline. Cable cars and electric trolleys became part of a massive mass transit system. What is more, Chicago was prepared to show itself to the world and did so during the World's Columbian Exposition in 1893. *White City*, as

A view of Chicago immediately after the great fire of 1871

the planned exposition ground was called, was visited by some 27,000,000 people—an extraordinary number—between May and October.

In 1909 Daniel H. Burnham, who had been chief architect of *White City,* unveiled his *Plan for Chicago.* The plan called for an improved waterfront, a new highway system, the consolidation of railroad facilities, the widening of major streets, and a modern park system. In the years that followed much of the *Plan for Chicago* was implemented.

And the city continued to grow. In 1910 Chicago's population stood at over 2,000,000; in 1930 it was well over 3,000,000. The city's population peaked in 1950 at 3,620,962. It has been declining slightly ever since. In 1980, it was 3,005,072. Over 7,000,000 however, live in the Chicago Metropolitan Area.

The city of the present day is an important manufacturing community. Chicago makes radios, TV sets, telephone equipment, and machinery. It produces chemicals and transportation equipment. To perform these tasks, millions of tons of iron ore, coal, chemicals, oil, lumber, and farm products must be brought to the city.

Today shoppers can use the Magnificent Mile—luxury retail stores, hotels, office buildings—along Michigan Avenue. Since 1975 they have had access to Water Tower Place—74 stories high—with the stores Marshall Field and Lord and Taylor, located there. State Street has always been a popular shopping location.

For the Chicagoan and the tourist alike, Chicago is replete with magnificent museums, art galleries, educational establish-

The Chicago skyline
from Lake Shore Drive

ments, and recreational facilities. It is a first-rate convention center. It has a new skyline. The First National Bank Building, the John Hancock Center, and the Sears Tower—the world's tallest building, with 110 stories—from which one can view the entire city and more.

Like other large cities Chicago has many problems. Crime, poverty, and segregation are among them. But it also has the *Comprehensive Plan of Chicago* (1966) designed to guide the growth of the city into the 1980s. The Comprehensive Plan was designed with human and economic needs in mind—with quality of life, opportunities for the disadvantaged, with jobs, and the movement of goods and services.

In a city which is only 40 percent black the people elected a black man, Harold Washington, mayor in 1983.

DETROIT

Detroit is older than Chicago. It was founded as a fort by Antoine de la Mothe Cadillac in 1701. Log cabins, a church, a warehouse, and a public bake house soon occupied the site. The local Indians moved their villages close by for protection and trade. Unfortunately Cadillac left in 1711 and the site deteriorated.

In 1760 the British took over. During the Revolutionary War there were as many as 300 troops quartered in the fort. In 1778 they began construction of a new fort. And while they were supposed to leave Detroit in 1783 (Treaty of Paris) they remained until 1796. At the time most of the people in Detroit were French (former soldiers, traders, and farmers). There were also the British (officials, landowners, merchants, and traders) and a sprinkling of Dutch, Germans, and Americans (only those loyal to the King).

People began to come to the community in increasing numbers. By 1805, Detroit was an American community. When the

Michigan Territory was created in 1805, Detroit was made the capital. In the same year, however, the village caught fire and every building save one was burned to the ground.

The village was rebuilt. In the War of 1812 the Americans surrendered the site. The British occupied it for over a year only to relinquish it to American troops on September 29, 1813.

With the opening of the Erie Canal and the establishment of a land office in Detroit, the little community began to grow. In 1830 Detroit's population was 2,222; by 1850 it was 21,019. At mid-century there were 10,000 foreigners in the city (from Ireland, the German Empire, England, Wales, and Scotland). Woodward Avenue had become the chief artery. There was a growing commercial and industrial base. City manufacturers were building wagons and carriages, ships, and furniture. Before long Detroit was making railroad cars, working in metals, iron and steel, copper and brass. Manufacturers were making paints and pills and stoves. For fifty years the manufacture of stoves was the city's leading industry.

The horsecar carried the inhabitants farther away from the city's center; after 1886 the electric railroad enabled the Detroiter to commute over even longer distances. By 1900 Detroit's population stood at 285,704. The city had its large German population, its Polish community, its Russian and Polish Jews, and its small number of blacks (only 4,111 in 1900) along St. Antoine.

In 1899 Ransom E. Olds had established Detroit's first automobile plant. Henry Ford built the Ford Motor Company in 1903. By 1908 he was turning out the Model T. In 1913, at the Highland Park plant, he set in motion the first automotive assembly line. And on January 14, 1914 Ford let it be known that each of his production workers would be paid at the then fantastic rate of $5.00 for an eight-hour work day. The job seekers streamed to Detroit.

It has been boom or near bust ever since. In 1929 the automobile industry produced 5.3 million cars; in 1931—a Great Depression year—only 1.3 million. Many people were out of work. Detroit recovered during World War II as the city became the "Arsenal of Democracy." Chrysler made more than its quota of tanks, Hudson its navy guns, and Ford turned out 8,500 B-24 Liberator bombers at Willow Run. The war brought many blacks and southern whites to the Motor City. The city's population had leaped to 1,623,452 in 1940 and, like Chicago's, had peaked in 1950 at 1,849,568.

The 1950s and 60s were prosperous years. The automobile industry turned out an astonishing 9,300,000 units in 1965. It looked as if the sky was the limit. But in 1967 the city was devastated by the race riot (looting, arson, and sniping) and 12th Street was left in shambles. In the 1970s automobile production slowed once more. Yet Detroit was able to show a new face to the world with the completion of the Renaissance Center in 1977. But in the early 1980s unemployment in Detroit went to 17 percent. The automobile industry was struggling. And people were beginning to wonder if the Motor City could survive on the automobile, or whether or not it would have to make new and different plans for the future.

OTHER CITIES

Cleveland and Cincinnati, Ohio; Indianapolis and Fort Wayne Indiana; Peoria and East St. Louis, Illinois; Grand Rapids and Saginaw, Michigan; Milwaukee and Kenosha, Wisconsin; Minneapo-

Symbol of rebirth—
Detroit's Renaissance Center

Other major cities of the North Central
states include Milwaukee, Wisconsin
(left) and Bismarck, North Dakota, whose
state capitol building is nicknamed
"Skyscraper of the Prairies" (above).

lis and Mankato, Minnesota; St. Louis and Kansas City, Missouri; Topeka, Kansas; Omaha, Nebraska; Pierre and Bismarck, in the Dakotas, are all cities of the American Heartland. They grew as America grew, as the American Heartland matured. They helped to create the American Heartland; they are all reflections of it.

American Heartland cities have survived boom and near bust, but today they face, perhaps, their greatest challenge. How will they cope in the late 1980s, the 1990s, and the opening years of the twenty-first century?

THE FUTURE

Cheap land and freedom had lured American settler-farmers westward. They hacked fields from the forest and planted corn on the prairie. In time they came to grips with the dry plains and planted wheat from Kansas to the Dakotas. In Wisconsin a Dairyland was born.

The settler-farmers, isolated from the manufacturing areas in the East, began to manufacture their own goods. They made their own salt, sawed their own lumber, distilled their own whiskey, and brewed their own beer. They worked in iron, made boots and shoes, carts and wagons, furniture and agricultural implements.

And whether they farmed, worked in home or factory, or did some other community service, they came to possess an important set of values. They lived by hard work; they admired the self-made person, they liked efficiency and progress. They prospered and so did their descendants.

There were, of course, periods of gloom and despair. Today the American Heartland is in the midst of a difficult period. There are troubles on the farms, in the factories, and in the cities. Unemployment is high. The job picture is so poor that people have been leaving the American Heartland for the Sun Belt and other areas, where jobs may be easier to find.

The challenge seems quite clear. The American Heartland must modernize—on farm, in factory, and in city alike. It must use its natural and human resources to their fullest, to recover, to compete and lead itself—and perhaps the nation—out of the doldrums.

The iron, steel, and automobile industries are already retooling. They are turning to robots. They are placing new emphases on quality and productivity. There is little question that their performance is critical for the future well-being of the American Heartland. At the same time, the "new" industries—computers, electronics, communications, and microbiology—the so-called "hi-techs," are booming and growing. So, too, are the service industries. They, too, will make an enormous difference in what the future holds for the American Heartland.

Accordingly there is need for retraining and new training for new and different jobs. And there is need for new thinking. The American Heartland has a most important resource, for example, in the world's largest supply of fresh water—the Great Lakes. Obviously the Great Lakes must be kept clean. They must be protected from pollution. In the very near future, there will undoubtedly be many calls for Great Lakes water—especially from the dry areas in the Sun Belt. It may be possible to pipe water from Lake Superior to the Mississippi River, 160 miles (257 km) away, or

One of the ways automobile manufacturers are hoping to get the industry back on its feet is through new technology and equipment, like the industrial robots in this Ford plant.

to the Missouri River, 400 miles (644 km) away. The American Heartland may be able to sell its water—at a huge profit—to the western and southwestern states. Or, it may be used by the farmers in the American Heartland itself, and to attract more jobs and industries to the area.

The American Heartland emerged in the nineteenth century. It prospered in its mechanized agriculture and in its thriving iron and steel industry. It grew powerful in the twentieth century on the shoulders of the automobile, and mightier with the introduction of the soybean and the development of hybrid corn. The American Heartland became the breadbasket of the nation and even helped to feed the world.

Today the American Heartland is in a difficult period. But it has already put its shoulders to the wheel to create in Ohio, Indiana, Illinois, Michigan, Wisconson, Minnesota, Iowa, Missouri, Nebraska, Kansas, South Dakota, and North Dakota a new, a better, and an even more prosperous area—one that really deserves to be called the American Heartland—in the not-too-distant future.

STATE
FACTS

ILLINOIS

year admitted to Union: 1818
capital: Springfield
nickname: Land of Lincoln
motto: "State sovereignty, national union"
flower: Meadow violet
bird: Eastern cardinal
song: "Illinois"
flag: Emblem similar to state seal in color on a white field.
    "Illinois" appears under the emblem.

INDIANA

year admitted to Union: 1816
capital: Indianapolis
nickname: Hoosier State
motto: "The Crossroads of America"
flower: Peony
bird: Cardinal

song: "On the Banks of the Wabash Far Away"
flag: A gold burning torch surrounds two circles of golden stars.
The star above the flame represents Indiana.

IOWA

year admitted to Union: 1846
capital: Des Moines
nickname: Hawkeye State
motto: "Our liberties we prize and our rights we will maintain"
flower: Wild rose
bird: Eastern goldfinch
song: "The Song of Iowa"
flag: Red, white, and blue vertical stripes. An eagle at the center
carries the state motto. "Iowa" appears below the eagle.

KANSAS

year admitted to Union: 1861
capital: Topeka
nickname: Sunflower State
motto: "To the stars through difficulties"
flower: Sunflower
bird: Western meadowlark
song: "Home on the Range"
flag: The state seal is in the center on a blue field.
"Kansas" appears near the bottom in gold letters.

MICHIGAN

year admitted to Union: 1837
capital: Lansing
nickname: Wolverine State

motto: "If you seek a pleasant peninsula, look about you"
flower: Apple blossom
bird: Robin
song: "Michigan, My Michigan"
flag: The state coat of arms appears on a deep blue field.

MINNESOTA

year admitted to Union: 1858
capital: Saint Paul
nickname: Gopher State
motto: "The star of the north"
flower: Showy lady's slipper
bird: Loon
song: "Hail! Minnesota"
flag: The state seal is shown in the center of a deep blue field. Surrounding the seal is a white band containing nineteen stars—the nineteenth representing Minnesota. The year of statehood is indicated (1858); so is the year of the erection of Fort Snelling (1819); and the year the flag was adopted (1893).

MISSOURI

year admitted to Union: 1821
capital: Jefferson City
nickname: The "Show Me" State
motto: "Let the welfare of the people be the supreme law"
flower: Hawthorn
bird: Bluebird
song: "Missouri Waltz"
flag: Three horizontal bands—red, white, and blue. The state coat of arms is in the center.

NEBRASKA

year admitted to Union: 1869
capital: Lincoln
nickname: Cornhusker State
motto: "Equality before the law"
flower: Goldenrod
bird: Western meadowlark
song: "Beautiful Nebraska"
flag: Includes the seal colored in silver and blue
    in the center of a field of national blue.

NORTH DAKOTA

year admitted to Union: 1889
capital: Bismarck
nickname: Flickertail State
motto: "Liberty and union, now and forever,
    one and inseparable"
flower: Wild prairie rose
bird: Western meadowlark
song: "North Dakota Hymn"
flag: At the center is the eagle, the national emblem. The national
    motto appears on a streamer in the eagle's beak. Thirteen
    stars are above the eagle's head. "North Dakota" appears on a
    scroll below the eagle.

OHIO

year admitted to Union: 1803
capital: Columbus
nickname: Buckeye State
motto: "With God all things are possible"

flower: Scarlet carnation
bird: Cardinal
song: "Beautiful Ohio"
flag: A pennant-shaped flag with red and white stripes. At the staff
    end is a blue triangle in which seventeen white stars are
    grouped around a white circle with a red center. The white
    circle represents the first letter in Ohio; the red center repre-
    sents the buckeye seed.

SOUTH DAKOTA

year admitted to Union: 1889
capital: Pierre
nickname: Sunshine State
motto: "Under God the people rule"
flower: Pasqueflower
bird: Ring-necked pheasant
song: "Hail! South Dakota"
flag: The state seal is surrounded by a sunburst in a field of blue.
    "South Dakota" and its nickname, "Sunshine State" surround
    the sunburst.

WISCONSIN

year admitted to Union: 1848
capital: Madison
nickname: Badger State
motto: "Forward"
flower: Violet
bird: Robin
song: "On, Wisconsin"
flag: The coat of arms appears on both sides of a dark blue flag.

INDEX